Looking at Life Cycles

Daisy

Victoria Huseby

A⁺
Smart Apple Media

Smart Apple Media is published by Black Rabbit Books
P.O. Box 3263, Mankato, Minnesota 56002

Printed in the United States

Published by arrangement with the Watts Publishing Group Ltd, London.

Editor: Rachel Tonkin
Designer: Proof Books
Picture researcher: Diana Morris
Science consultant: Andrew Solway
Literacy consultant: Gill Matthews
Illustrations: John Alston

Picture credits:
Niall Benvie/OSF: 11; John Crellin/Photographers Direct: 17b, 21; Holt Studios/FLPA Images: 7, 19;
Sally Morgan/Ecoscene: 9; Opla/Shutterstock: 15; Photogenes: 4; Emilia Stasiak/Shutterstock: 13;
Emma Tumman/Photographers Direct: front cover; Craig Tuttle/Corbis: 1, 5

Library of Congress Cataloging-in-Publication Data

Huseby, Victoria.
    Daisy / by Victoria Huseby.
    p. cm.—(Smart Apple Media. Looking at life cycles)
    Summary: "An introduction to the life cycle of a daisy from seed to flower"—
Provided by publisher.
    Includes index.
    ISBN 978-1-59920-179-5
    1. Daisies—Life cycles—Juvenile literature. I. Title.
QK495.C74H87 2009
583'.99—dc22
                                                                    2007030466

9 8 7 6 5 4 3 2 1

Contents

Seed

A daisy is a plant with **flowers** that grows in fields and gardens. It grows from a tiny **seed**.

Daisy seeds

actual size $1/8$ inch (3 mm)

4

Shoot

In spring, the seed
begins to grow in the
soil. A **shoot** grows up
out of the seed. Leaves
grow from the shoot.

7

Flower

When the daisy is one or two weeks old, it grows a flower. The flower has white **petals** and a yellow **flower head** at its center.

9

Nighttime

At night, when it is dark,
the daisy's flower closes up.
In the morning, when it
is light, the flower opens
up again.

Nectar

During the day, **insects** visit the daisy's flower to drink the sweet **nectar** that it makes.

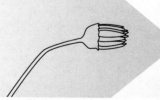

Pollen

As the insect drinks the nectar, yellow **pollen** from the daisy sticks to it. The insect then flies off to visit another daisy.

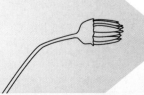

Pollination

The insect moves the pollen
from the first daisy to
the new daisy. The new
daisy is now **pollinated**.
It can grow seeds.

New Seeds

After the daisy has been pollinated, its petals drop off. Seeds form in the yellow flower head.

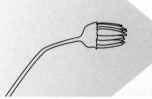

New Flowers

Some seeds fall to the ground. Others are blown away in the wind or carried away by animals. The seeds lie in the soil all winter. In spring, new daisies grow.

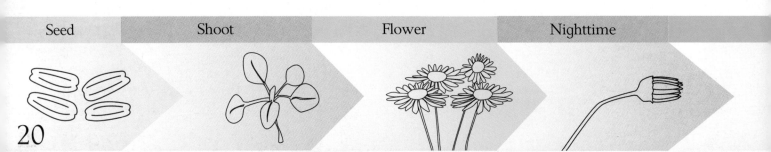

Seed   Shoot   Flower   Nighttime

 Nectar

 Pollination

 New Seeds

 New Flowers

21

Daisy Facts

- The name daisy probably comes from "day's eye," because the daisy's flower opens during the day and closes at night.

- Plants are given scientific names in Latin. The Latin name for a daisy is "Bellis." It means pretty.

- Daisies were once used as medicine. They were called "bruisewort" because they were believed to be good for healing bruises.

- Daisies come from the biggest family of flowering plants in the world. There are around 20,000 different kinds of daisies.

Glossary

Flower
The part of the plant that makes seeds.

Flower head
The middle part of the flower where seeds form.

Insects
Animals with six legs and two antennae, or feelers.

Nectar
Sweet liquid found in flowers.

Petals
The colored parts of a flower.

Pollen
A powder found in the flowers of plants. Pollen must be moved from one plant to another for new seeds to form.

Pollinated
When pollen has been moved from one flower to another and a flower can grow new seeds.

Seed
The part of a plant that grows to make a new plant.

Shoot
The first growth of a young plant above the ground. Shoot also means any new growth, such as a bud or branch, from a plant.

Soil
The earth that plants grow in.

Index and Web Sites

For Kids:

BrainPOP Jr.: Plant Life Cycle
http://www.brainpopjr.com/science/
plants/plantlifecycle/

The Great Plant Escape
http://www.urbanext.uiuc.edu/gpe/

Plants at Enchanted Learning
http://www.enchantedlearning.com/
themes/plants.shtml

For Teachers:

**Introduction: Life Cycle of a
Flowering Plant**
http://www.teachnet.ie/leahy/
introduction.htm

Teachers' Domain: Plant Life Cycles
http://www.teachersdomain.org/resources
/tdc02/sci/life/colt/lp_plantcycle